I *of the* Garden

My dear sister Ayport!

May Allah bless you always!

In the name of God, *the* Lord of Mercy,
the Giver of Mercy ...

I *of the* Garden

CYRUS MCGOLDRICK

Muslim Renaissance Group

Cover art painted and photographed by Sarosh Arif
www.Arneeq.org

First printing: February 2014 / Rabi al-Thani 1435

ISBN-13: 978-0615958217
ISBN-10: 0615958214

Muslim Renaissance Group
www.MuslimRenaissance.com

With glad tidings for the strangers …

Episodes —

I.   Far from the Tree
II.   Red Gold
III.   Prisms
IV.   Shudder
V.   Violet
VI.   Soil
VII.   Genesis

Strike the shepherd,
and the sheep will be scattered.

Zachariah 13:7, *The Bible*

You talk when you cease to be at peace with your
thoughts.

Khalil Gibran, *The Prophet*

I of the Garden |

I –

Far from the Tree

I of the Garden |

1 –

Illustrate! Visions
Cut from heavenly clusters
Petals and clutter

I of the Garden |

2 –

Tempting testaments
Sending sensual lessons
Mentioning blessings
Sleep is for dead men
Beautiful women instead
Resting red tears shed

I of the Garden |

3 –

Sweat dries in the breeze
Alone under suns not free
Blown far from the tree
Thrown in the machine
Bleeding leeches riding dreams
Feeding silent needs
Lost in chemistry
Elements and centuries
Love and felonies

I of the Garden |

4 –

Flower peddling
Hiding from our skeletons
Sunshine settles in
One more direction
Message sent from the censors
Don't mention weapons
Chess sets not checkers
Swift desperate endeavors
Lists left defenseless
Slept in December
Letters sent to two mentors
Celestial ventures

I of the Garden |

5 –

Thinking of actions
Friction and exact fractions
Steady extraction
Seasonal chasms
Summer shoes and a jacket
Raindrops and laughing
Valleys and bad ruts
Deep shadows and shallow cuts
Buds and lasting lust
Love like winter suns
Turning but always burning
Yearning for the one
Songs of caged birds
Echoed by migrating flocks
Learned on lonely docks

I of the Garden |

II –

Red Gold

I of the Garden |

6 -

Light rain and flowers
Healing eight painful powers
Leaning steel towers
Loving lost hours
Fields that some men pay to plow
They are never ours
Wet words and lost towns
Flowers fed by broken clouds
Mountains of soft pounds
Pain and happy sounds
Blind wise men drip solemn vows
Whispers counting down

I of the Garden |

7 –

Founts of young recruits
Found underground astounding
Death in living truths
The uprooted shoots
An executioner's noose
Thistles and thick roots
Liquor and stiff boots
Stained juice of low hanging fruits
Scarred by broken tooth

I of the Garden |

8 –

Killing all feeling
Hide heat behind steel ceilings
Eat off your stealing
Bloody battlefields
Bent knees and somber blue tones
Lost friends and left foes

I of the Garden |

9 –

Squeezing blood from stones
Wheels and poems lurch and groan
Twelve tribes hide from drones

I of the Garden |

10 –

Motions and love potions
Antidotes to poisoned jokes
Oceans foiling boats
Soft translucent robes
Slowly loosen an old foe
Lost bones and tossed phones
One loose thread left holes
Whole worlds dead when cold coal bled
Low slow murmurs spread
Never whole alone
Walk unknown streets of red gold
Sentries have gone cold
Entries to lost folds
One soul stood as one before
Die before you go

I of the Garden |

III –

Prisms

I of the Garden |

11 –

Fighting divisions
Finding light in blind prisms
Divining wisdoms
Riding on rhythms
True visions distilled missions
Disciplined sit-ins

I of the Garden |

12 –

Perfect signed finding
Colonized minds colliding
Lion pride hunting time
Sighs and sweet fires
Cutting wood for final pyres
High on cable wires
Hyenas crying
Finding wild hide left behind
Lies with steady eyes

I of the Garden |

13 –

Death in the first line
Rewind and find a blank time
Red pens on white minds
Worlds turned in soft eyes
Tested in both deaths and lives
Blunt ends and sharp knives

I of the Garden |

14 –

Blind to sense's signs
Find dimensions between lines
Truths unwind in time

I of the Garden |

15 –

Find fruits lining vines
Trusting kind angelic signs
Smoke signs and red pines
Diamonds in coal mines
Shepherds compete to end time
Bent horizons rise

I of the Garden |

IV –

Shudder

I of the Garden |

16 –

Tracing lines on thighs
Hearts sigh racing melodies
Sparks of art divine

I of the Garden |

17 –

Signed by nine blind minds
Light veils dark and lifts an ark
Nails charts and two larks
Start beating rhythms
Narcs charging darkened visions
Darts parting prisons

I of the Garden |

18 –

Charge hard where hearts met
Art can part cards and start them
Harps and tongues left stung
Shallow seeds far flung
Shadows showers and forked tongues
Flowers port unsung

I of the Garden |

19 –

Arms light wind and cup
Charms and regard stars above
Shudder and find love
Covered in colors
Perfectly finished puzzles
Wolves wearing muzzles

I of the Garden |

20 –

Half is not enough
Laughing thunder when it's rough
Lightning strikes up

I of the Garden |

V –

Violet

I of the Garden |

21 –

Beauty expected
Surviving by selection
Violent election
Vibrant collection
Left in bed with liberty
Direct connection
Die of affection
Unexploited voice noticed
Sexual moments

I of the Garden |

22 –

Roses with dry lips
Violet eyes and wide hips
Climbing by thin wits

I of the Garden |

23 –

Breaking through gun lines
Winding love to find hating
Next to and facing
Races and pacing
Chasing love raising nations
Patiently waiting
Our expectations
Flexible meditation
Learning in stages

I of the Garden |

24 –

Warm rain and sworn bases
Black lace torn in four places
Faces in mazes

I of the Garden |

25 –

Casing stern cages
Burning books and turning pages
Aged gray faced sages

I of the Garden |

VI –

Soil

I of the Garden |

26 –

A radical strikes
Reach into oil soil deep roots
True seeds' shoots breed fruit

I of the Garden |

27 –

Living hardly twice
Fire gardens and arctic nights
Spice at highest price
Icy roads remain
Broken chains take holy names
Vice changes old games

I of the Garden |

28 –

Lyrical affair
Spiritual serenades
Spears and hand grenades
Pictures without frames
Scripts with scriptural refrains
States and cryptic planes

I of the Garden |

29 –

Watching feathers fall
Plotting lots with walls vetted
Sprawling lawns wetted
Skins linked together
Weather fades for our bender
Tethered unfettered

I of the Garden |

30 –

Threatened by mirrors
Battling teams of demons
Shadows are clearer
Spliffs and old sweaters
Ski masks and young bank tellers
Left in simple flicks
Licks and shopping lists
Fists click clocking ticking bombs
Knowledge stitching wrists

I of the Garden |

VII –

Genesis

I of the Garden |

31 –

Two seasons to taste
Chase reason with a lime's face
Sun rays set time's pace

I of the Garden |

32 –

Shapes do not take lakes
Racing to fill empty space
Juries hang a case

I of the Garden |

33 –

For an Irish wake
Whiskey eulogies and steak
Dying lies in state

I of the Garden |

34 –

Shakes from foreign quakes
Ripples dripping across lakes
Faces and lost takes

I of the Garden |

35 –

Cake for a birthday
Snakes may not be metaphors
Genesis left more
Politics and war
Sores on fingertips of poor
Soldiers keeping score
Hearing rebel roars
Yelling ready for the Lord
Devil in the fore
Torn from dormant shores
I in the eye of the storm
While core gardens form
Floors torn by dark pours
Corps warm to forgotten norms
A fallen rock warns

I of the Garden |

The End —

I of the Garden |

I of the Garden |

About the Author —

CYRUS MCGOLDRICK

American of Iranian and Irish descent. Caller
to Islamic practice and social organization.
Community organizer, writer, musician,
speaker and radio host.

Previous works include: *The Raskol Khan: Past
to Present* (2013); *The New York Chapter* (2011),
with Freddy Gonzalez & the Fuego Xtet;
Street Kings – Election Day (2008) and *Transport
& Logistics* (2008), with Adrian Martin.

www.BrotherCyrus.com

I of the Garden |

About the Publisher –

MUSLIM RENAISSANCE GROUP

Strategic and organizational consulting for communities and charities. Artistic and academic production, publishing and distribution. Speakers bureau.

www.MuslimRenaissance.com

I of the Garden |

A Prayer –

IN THE NAME OF GOD, THE LORD OF MERCY,
THE GIVER OF MERCY …

We seek refuge in God from all evil, and bear
witness that there is nothing worthy of
worship except the Divine Source, the Lord
of all Power, the Writer and Creator and
Provider, Greater than whatever is associated
with Him. May His noble messengers and
righteous followers be showered with
blessings and peace, and may He guide us also
to lives in His service and love, lived
prophetically, struggling for good in this life
and the next.

Ameen.

I of the Garden |

I of the Garden |

I of the Garden |

31198342R00069

Made in the USA
Lexington, KY
02 April 2014